Bomber Planes

by Jay Schleifer

Capstone Press

MINNEAPOLIS

Printed in the United States of America.

Capstone Press • 2440 Fernbrook Lane • Minneapolis, MN 55447

Editorial Director   John Coughlan
Managing Editor   Tom Streissguth
Production Editor   James Stapleton
Book Design   Tim Halldin

Library of Congress Cataloging-in-Publication Data

J

Schleifer, Jay. 358.42
   Bomber planes / Jay Schleifer. Sch
      p. cm. -- (Wings)
   Includes bibliographical references (p. 46) and index.
   Summary: Describes the design of various types of
bombers, their uses in combat, and their role in the future.
   ISBN 1-56065-303-5
   1. Bombers--Juvenile literature. 2. Bombing, Aerial--
Juvenile literature. [1. Bombers. 2. Airplanes, Military.]
I. Title. II. Series: Wings (Minneapolis, Minn.)
   UG1242.B6S33   1996
   358.4'2--dc20   95-11245
                                                 CIP
                                                  AC

Table of Contents

Chapter 1
The Mission

The night is black as ink as your **bomber** closes in on a weapons factory in the heart of the enemy's homeland. If you do your job right, weapons will not be made there much longer.

As you gear up for battle, you know the enemy is waiting for you. They are searching for you on **radar**. Their **fighters** are already in the air. Hundreds of missiles and guns point skyward, waiting to bring down your plane.

Two B2 Stealth bombers take on fuel at an army desert airfield.

With landing gear extended, the USAF B-1 bomber prepares for a safe landing.

But the enemy doesn't know *how* you are coming. You will not arrive in a wave of huge, noisy planes that darken the sky like a cloud. Instead, you're flying a single plane that is as silent as the night–the B-2 **Stealth** bomber.

You sit at the controls, amazed at how easily the plane slices through enemy defenses. Though your plane is as big as a house, it looks as tiny as a bird on radar. You drift past the

fighters and over the missiles like a ghost. Suddenly you are over the target.

Of course, this run is just practice. Your "bomb" is a radio signal. Computers pick it up to measure how close you came to a bullseye. Later you will meet with the enemy back at the base and joke about who was "Top Gun" today.

But practice makes perfect, especially for bomber crews. If your nation is ever attacked, you and your B-2 will be ready.

Chapter 2

All About Bombers

The B-2 Stealth is the latest in a line of airplanes known as bombers. Bombers carry the war over the heads of enemy armies, right to their homeland. Bombers knock out the factories that make weapons and the roads and railways that carry them. They hit enemy armies and enemy cities. Some experts say that bombers can win a war without a single ground soldier firing a shot.

Not all bombers are alike. Long-range or heavy bombers deliver large weapons over

(Next page): A Boeing KC-135 refuels a B-1 Bomber in mid-flight.

Swept-back wings, a needle-point nose, and a compact design allow this bomber to fly nearly as fast as fighter planes.

thousands of miles. Medium bombers fly shorter distances at high speed. They're often used against an enemy's headquarters or to break up an enemy unit preparing for battle.

Attack planes (also called dive bombers or fighter/bombers) are the size of a fighter and almost as fast. They zoom in over the battlefield and hit single targets that are opposing friendly forces.

Bombers can also be used against ships. During World War II (1939-1945), the Japanese attacked Pearl Harbor, a naval base in Hawaii. Their bombers destroyed much of the American navy in a single raid.

Today's bombers carry missiles and **smart bombs** as well as the usual free-falling weapons. Missiles can be fired from a safe distance, sometimes from hundreds of miles away. A smart bomb can be steered as it falls. It can hit a single building, and even enter a single window of that building.

Bombers also carry the most terrible weapon ever, the nuclear bomb. This bomb explodes with the same energy that heats the sun. Just one nuclear bomb can kill a million people. These weapons were used against two cities in Japan during World War II. The bombings so upset humankind that they haven't been used in battle since. Some nations are destroying their **nuclear weapons** to be sure they're never used.

Chapter 3
Fortresses that Fly

Like other warplanes, the bomber was invented during World War I (1914-18). The first bombing attacks were carried out by pilots tossing explosives over the side of their planes. Before long, there were special planes with bomb holders under the wings. Some of these early bombers had an opening in the belly, called the **bomb bay**, for dropping explosives.

The larger the bomber, the more it carried. Bombers quickly became the biggest planes in the sky. Some had four or more engines, in a

A fire-control computer system helped make the B-29 Superfortress the first truly modern bomber.

day when even single-engine planes were rare. One of the largest bombers was called The Goliath.

The first bombers were not a success. Their engines produced little power, so the heavy planes could hardly get out of their own way. They were easy targets for fighters and ground fire. Bad weather could stop them. Even in good weather, there was no sure way to control the bombs. If the wind changed, they were as likely to hit friendly forces as the enemy.

For these reasons, most army leaders felt the bomber would never work. But General William "Billy" Mitchell believed in it. He took his case to the newspapers, where he wrote about the bomber's future as a weapon of war. Finally, in 1921, officials set up a test of the bomber's power. If it failed, Mitchell would be forced to quiet down.

Mitchell's planes were ordered to attack a giant battleship captured during the war. Navy officials felt that such ships were unsinkable.

Mitchell's planes flew over, dropping 2,000-pound (900-kilogram) bombs. The giant ship went to the bottom in just 22 minutes. Mitchell had proven his point.

Years later, a new bomber, the B-25, was named the Mitchell to honor the general for standing by his ideas. It was the first U.S. warplane to bomb Japan during World War II.

After Mitchell, the question was no longer whether to build bombers. It was how to build the best bomber. The Boeing Airplane Company came up with the answer.

The twin-engine B-25 was named the Mitchell after U.S. General William Mitchell.

Machine guns on the B-17's nose, tail, sides, and top and bottom protected the plane from enemy fighters.

Boeing Flying Fortress

In the 1930s, most bombers were two-engine craft with top speeds of barely 200 miles per hour. Bomb loads were less than a ton (900 kilograms).

That's when the Boeing Company decided to ignore the old designs. Their new B-17 was an all-metal, four-engine monster. It was one of the biggest planes ever built to that time.

Top speed was close to 300 miles (480 kilometers) per hour. The plane could carry twice the usual weight in bombs. And to keep fighters off, the B-17 carried up to 13 machine guns on its nose, tail, sides, top and bottom. In every way, the plane was a **Flying Fortress**–and that's just what Boeing called it.

Bomber crews often tattooed their flying ships with artwork and symbols showing the history of the plane in battle.

During World War II, nearly 13,000 B-17s were built. Most were used against Germany. The planes were sent out hundreds at a time, against heavy fire. The B-17 was a very tough airplane. A Flying Fortress could lose half a wing and most of its tail and still limp home. Nevertheless, many planes and their crews never came back.

The Superfortress

Meanwhile, Boeing was working on the next step. They called it the B-29 Superfortress.

These Superfortresses flew in the Pacific theater of operations during World War II.

Used against Japan, the B-29 was the first truly modern bomber. It was 25 feet (8 meters) longer than a B-17, and had wings 39 feet (12 meters) wider. A crew of 10 fired its guns with one of the first **fire control computers**.

The B-29's top speed was 363 miles (581 kilometers) per hour–faster than many of the fighters sent to shoot it down. It carried four times the bombs of a B-17. And it could fly six miles (10 kilometers) high. That was well above the top height most enemy fighters could fly.

Some of the hardest-hitting B-29 runs were at low level. Missions of 1,000 or more planes flew into Japan at rooftop height. They dropped **firebombs** on the wooden houses, and in one terrible night burned much of Tokyo.

There were other great bombers in the war, including the American B-24 and the British Lancaster, built with Canadian help. But the Superfortress finally ended the fighting. In 1945, B-29s dropped the first nuclear bombs on two Japanese cities. Just days later, Japan's leaders gave up.

Chapter 4
The Jet Threat

After the war, a new enemy arose. Russia, then part of the Soviet Union, had nuclear weapons, just as the U.S. did. The world held its breath as it watched these two superpowers face each other down.

To prevent a nuclear war, each nation tried to make the other believe a war was unwinnable. Each told the other that whoever hit first would be hit back and totally destroyed. The threat was backed with fleets of long-range bombers carrying nuclear weapons.

The American side flew the biggest warplane ever to fly–the B-36 Peacemaker. This plane had six propeller and four jet engines. It carried an incredible 72,000 pounds of bombs, nearly four times the load of a B-29. It was as long as a 23-story building is high. Its wings were so thick that crew members could walk inside them during a flight. To get from the nose to the tail, the crew chief drove a small car through a tunnel in the body.

Tractor type landing gear allowed the B-36 to land on unprepared runways.

Two USAF F-15s escort the Russian made Tupelov Tu-95 Bear.

The plane's top speed was 436 miles (698 kilometers) per hour. It could fly halfway around the world without stopping for fuel.

The Russians answered with their own giant, which Americans called the Bear. Its had four turboprop engines, which combine propeller and jet design. It also had swept wings. The

Bear remains the only plane in the world with props as well as swept wings.

Not as big as a B-36, the Bear was faster. Top speed was 550 miles (880 kilometers) per hour, and it also could fly halfway around the world. Its specialty was drifting in the skies for hour after hour. Bears are still used by the

Loaded with nuclear bombs, the B-52 was built to protect the U.S. during the Cold War.

Russians to track naval ships and submarines across the oceans.

In the 1950s, these planes were the giants of the skies. But they were replaced when something better–the jet bomber–came along.

Boeing B-52

The U.S. Air Force calls it the B-52. Pilots call it the **BUF**, for Big Ugly Friend. By any name, this eight-engine plane has been one of

the world's top bombers for more than 40 years.

The plane has carried out many different missions. Its first job was replacing the B-36 as the plane that would hit back if the U.S. was ever attacked.

In this role, B-52s patrolled the skies over Canada and Alaska with nuclear bombs on board. The crew flew in great circles, waiting for a signal they hoped would never come. The signal would tell them to head for Russia.

Nearly as big as the lumbering B-36, the B-52 was as fast as a fighter jet: 650 miles (1,040 kilometers) per hour. Its bomb bays held at least four nuclear bombs, and it could carry them 12,500 miles (20,000 kilometers) before refueling was needed.

When the U.S. entered the **Vietnam** War, the BUF got a new job. B-52s were loaded with regular bombs and sent to drop them on enemy units in the jungles.

The enemy struck back with ground-to-air missiles. That's when crews found out that the

BUF was tough. Some B-52s made it home with half their engines on fire and their wings shot out.

By the 1980s, most other 1950s planes were long gone to the scrap heap. But the BUF got another mission as a low-level bomber. Crews flew this plane at the treetops, where radar couldn't see it. They dashed in at 400 miles (640 kilometers) per hour, fired missles, and got out.

B-52s are still flown in this role today. Many believe this plane will remain important well into the 21st century.

Chapter 5
Swing Wings and ICBMs

In the 1960s, many bombers were taken out of service by missiles. The missiles didn't actually bring down the planes. Instead, they took the bombers' job away.

The missile that put the most bomber crews out of work was the **ICBM** (intercontinental ballistic missile). From its silo, the ICBM could be fired at a moment's notice and reach

Swing wings allow the FB-111 to either reach top speeds at high altitudes or to fly close to the ground and dodge radar.

its target halfway around the world in half an hour. Bombers would take half a day for the same mission. The missile flew at 25,000 miles (40,000 kilometers) per hour, and nothing could stop it. It seemed like the perfect weapon.

But the ICBM had a weakness. Once launched, it could not be called back. Even if leaders changed their mind about fighting. Even if somebody launched it by mistake. Once someone pushed the firing button, the war was on. When world leaders understood this, they decided to keep some bombers too.

Aircraft designers were happy to make new bombers. But war had changed. New planes had to be able to fly lower than radar could see. They had to launch missiles as well as drop bombs. And they had to fight well in small wars as well as in a big one. In other words, any new bomber had to be several planes in one.

Swing-Wing Bombers

One new type of bomber had a **swing wing**–one that can be moved in flight. Flying low or slow, the plane's wings swing straight out for lots of lift. At supersonic speeds, they sweep back so the plane slips smoothly through the air.

The first U.S. bomber with these wings was a medium bomber called the F-111 Aardvark. It was followed by a heavy bomber, the Rockwell B-1B Lancer. Smaller than a B-52, the Lancer has a top speed of close to 1,000 miles (1,600 kilometers) per hour. Its four engines kick out

The Rockwell B-1 bomber's sandy camouflage blends in with the desert below.

30,000 pounds (13,500 kilograms) of **thrust** each. That is almost twice the power of a B-52. The B-1B's payload is amazing: 84 regular bombs, 24 nuclear bombs, or up to 24 missiles. Each Lancer can almost fight a war all on its own.

F-111s and B-1Bs have a **terrain-following radar** that reads the ground as the plane flies at treetop height. When the radar sees a hill, it causes the plane to rise. In a valley, the plane flies lower. It all happens without the pilot having to touch the controls.

Russia has two swing-wing bombers, which U.S. experts call the Backfire and the Blackjack. Americans got a close look at the Backfire when one flew over North America, probably to see if U.S. or Canadian radar could spot it. Fighters met this visitor and gently guided it back out over the ocean.

The Blackjack was first spotted in Russia by a spy satellite. Bigger than the B-1B, the Blackjack is the largest bomber of its kind ever built. Much about it is still secret.

This B-1 bomber proudly displays the "Penetrator" emblem.

But the Blackjack is not as secret as it once was. In the last few years, U.S. and Russian leaders have become more friendly. They've even visited each other's air bases. One news picture shows a top U.S. general sitting in the pilot's seat of a Blackjack.

In the picture, several Russians look worried about the Americans looking over their new plane. But other Russians are smiling. They may know that there's less chance of war now, and that the plane may never fly a deadly mission.

Chapter 6

The Plane That Isn't There

The U.S. and Russia may never fight, but other nations, such as Iraq, have started wars. Bombers still patrol the skies. And no matter who the enemy is, the planes still have to escape their biggest enemy–radar.

Radar is a means of locating airplanes in flight. An antenna shoots a beam of electrical energy into the sky. When the energy hits a

Three Stealth bombers fly over mountainous terrain.

The B-2's "flying wing" shape makes it look like an alien ship or a UFO (unidentified flying object).

plane, some of it bounces back. The radar unit measures this echo and shows the plane as a moving dot on a screen. The operator can then tell fighters and missiles where to find the plane.

The B-2 is a new bomber that can face the challenge of radar. Its weird shape scatters radar beams instead of bouncing them back. The special materials used to make the plane soak up radar beams, just as a sponge soaks up water. As a result, the beam never returns to the radar receiver. The enemy doesn't see the plane until the bombs fall.

The B-2 uses other tricks to sneak through to its target. Some ground-to-air missiles can follow engine heat, so the B-2's hot exhaust is

The Stealth Bomber's computer-generated shape allows it to fly almost totally undetected by radar.

Each Stealth bomber costs a half-billion dollars.

mixed with cool outside air as it exits. The four engines are buried in the body to keep the plane quiet. Special radios create static that jams enemy radar. Even the paint job helps hide the plane. The B-2 is the exact color of the night sky.

Because the B-2 has no tail, its flight can be unsteady. But computers constantly work the controls so the plane stays level. The Stealth has more than 200 computers on board. That's one reason each Stealth costs about $500 million. It's the most costly bomber ever built.

Do the tricks work? No B-2 has never flown in battle. But the F-117 Stealth fighter has. In a recent Mideast war, it was able to dart right into the center of the enemy's capital city. Nobody saw it coming.

Such a plane might make an enemy leader think twice before starting a war. And since the goal is to prevent war, that would make the B-2 successful, even if it never fires a shot.

Glossary

bomb bay–the space in a bomber's body that holds weapons. The weapons are dropped out through the bomb-bay door.

bomber–an airplane designed to carry weapons and drop them on enemy ground targets or ships

Onlookers admire this fully rebuilt B-29 bomber shown at an aircraft show in Oshkosh, Wisconsin.

BUF–the nickname for the B-52 heavy bomber. BUF stands for "Big Ugly Friend."

fighter–a small, fast warplane designed to shoot down other planes

firebomb–a special bomb designed to set targets afire as well as blow them up

fire control computer–a device that tracks and directs gunfire at enemy fighter planes

Flying Fortress–the nickname of the Boeing B-17, a World War II bomber

ICBM (intercontinental ballistic missile)–a long-range guided rocket that can deliver nuclear weapons at distances up to 5,000 miles (8,000 kilometers)

nuclear weapon–a bomb or missile that uses as an explosive the energy that heats the sun. Nuclear weapons are the most dangerous weapons ever made. One bomb can destroy a city.

radar–a system for locating planes in flight. Radar works by sending an electronic beam into the air that bounces back when crossed by an aircraft. Computers then read the echo for the location.

smart bomb–a bomb that can be steered as it falls, either by radio or through a long wire that unrolls from the plane

stealth–a system that makes a plane hard to track in the sky. Stealth technology includes an aircraft shape that scatters radar beams; materials that soak them up; extra-quiet engines; and exhaust gas coolers.

terrain-following radar–a system that allows a bomber to follow the outline of the ground as it seeks to avoid radar through low-level flight.

swing wing–a movable wing that can be adjusted in flight. Set straight out, the wing gives the plane more lift. Swept back, it allows higher speeds.

thrust–the measure of power of a jet engine. Thrust is measured in pounds of pressure the engine's exhaust would push against a surface.

Vietnam–a nation in Southeast Asia. The United States fought a war there in the 1960's and early 1970s.

To Learn More

Baker, Dr. David. *Bombers*. Vero Beach, Florida: Rourke Publishing Group, 1989.

Cooke, David C. *Famous U.S. Air Force Bombers*. New York: Dodd, Mead & Company, 1973.

Scott, Bill. *Inside the Stealth Bomber*. Blue Ridge Summit, Pennsylvania: TAB/Aero Books, 1991.

Taylor, Michael. *Jet Bombers*. Greenwich, Connecticut: Bison Books, 1983.

Walker, Bryce. *Fighting Jets*. New York: Time-Life Books, 1983

Some Useful Addresses

National Air and Space Museum
6th Street and Independence Avenue
Washington, DC 20560

United States Air Force Museum
Wright-Patterson Air Force Base, OH 45433
(Located near Dayton, OH)

New England Air Museum
Bradley International Airport
Windsor Locks, CT 06096

National Aviation Museum
P.O. Box 9724
Ottawa, Ontario, Canada KIG 543

Index